One Dot

Megan Godwin

Dedicated to my wonderful husband Roger Godwin. Thank you for always encouraging me to do the things I love.

One Dot: by Megan Godwin

ISBN: 9798817120653

One Dot

Megan Godwin

One dot.

One orange dot.

One orange dot here.

One orange dot there.

One orange dot below.

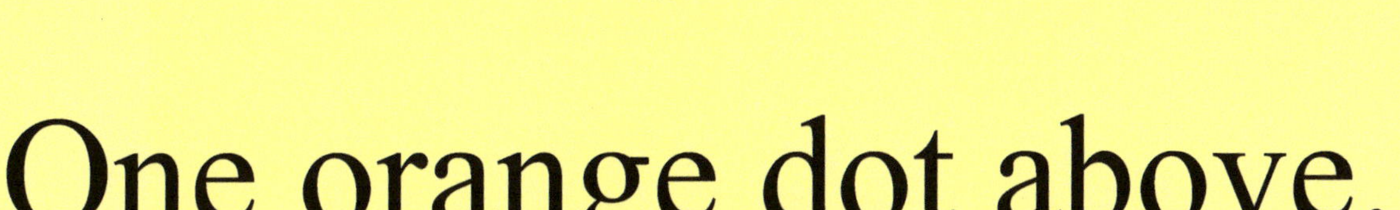

One orange dot above.

One orange
dot beside. 

One orange **dot** behind.

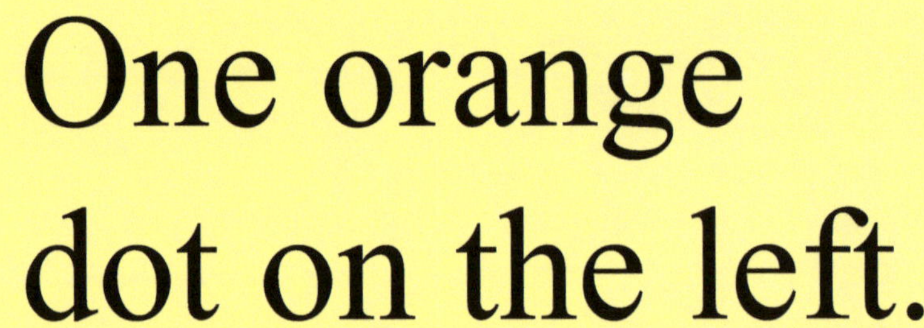

One orange
dot on the left.

One orange dot
on the right.

One orange dot at the top.

One orange dot at the
bottom.

One orange dot at the
bottom left corner.

One orange dot at the top right corner.

One orange dot inside.

One orange dot outside.

One orange dot on the chair.

One orange dot off the chair.

One orange dot close to the line.

One orange dot far from the line.

One orange dot upside down.

One orange dot right side
up.

One orange dot at the start.

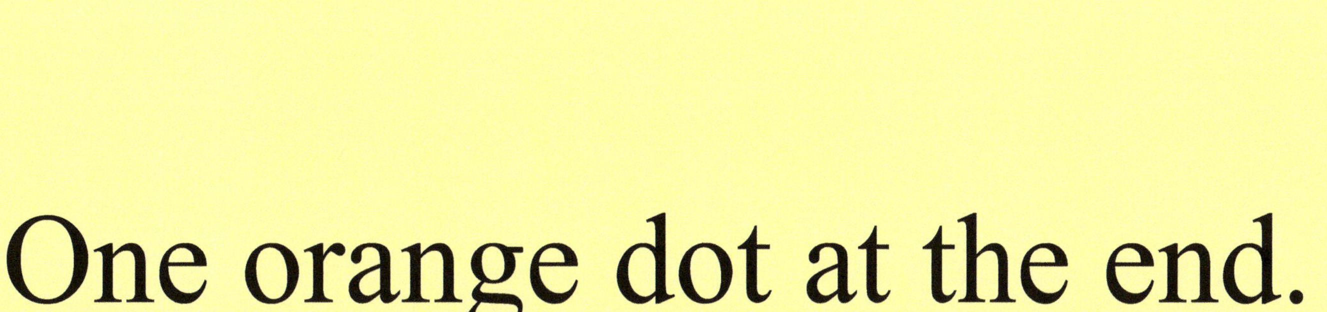

One orange dot at the end.

One orange dot.

One purple dot.

One orange dot and one
purple dot.

The End